<u>LATE NIGHT</u> <u>THOUGHTS Part 1</u>
by Kai Alexandria

Diving deep into the mind of a poet
to uncover the traumas, wonders
and secrets that lie beneath the
surface

Cover Art by: Kristin Lehner
https://www.facebook.com/Krissie-Junes-
Tattoos

Digital Work by:
Lindsay Heider Diamond

Warning:
This book is intended for mature readers. This
book contains explicit contents of sexual
language/situations, sexual abuse and mental
health issues that some readers may find
disturbing or triggering. Please read with
caution and at your own risk.

ISBN: 9781072422327

PREFACE:

Words, and the power that they hold. To heal, hurt, break, build, create, manifest and to change…

For a long time, I felt like my words meant nothing, so I kept them bottled up inside. I feared that speaking my truth would make me look like a fool, victim or make me sound stupid & ignorant. But let's be honest, we've all felt these things at some point or another in our lives. No matter how old we are, no one knows it all.

A lot of the time we feel we're unrelatable. That no one has been through what we've been through. That no one could possibly understand how we feel. So, we shy away from our truth and confine ourselves in a bubble. We don't want to be judged, ostracized, misunderstood or ridiculed. We quickly forget that we're all humans. We all have a story. We only show the bits & pieces that we want the world & people to see. No one is free from life's chaos no matter how "perfect" their life may look on the outside.

In my journey of life & writing this book, I've learned just how detrimental and toxic keeping everything inside can be. It led me down a very unhealthy and destructive path for many years, but thankfully I came out on the other side. The truth hurts, sometimes too much, but it must be faced in order to grow, heal, accept and move forward in life. I've learned to find beauty in pain, truth in confusion and that it's okay to not have it all together all the time.

I wrote this book for my own healing, understanding and release. But there came a turning point where I realized my words weren't meant for just me anymore. I pray that this book inspires & empowers people to heal, love, forgive, accept, learn about themselves & believe in themselves.

There's broken pieces, scratches, bruises and scars within all of us. I'm no longer afraid of my past, my pain, being happy, falling in love or being human. This book is me, my truth, my life on paper in all of its essence and beauty. So here I am, giving it all to you.

Contents

Chapter 1
Trauma & Heartbreak

"I filled you with love… and you left me
empty. Waiting to be fulfilled"

Life Without You

In the blink of an eye
You suddenly vanished
Life without you all these years
Not sure how I've managed
At a loss of emotions and words
Losing you caused unspeakable damage
A light in my life
Gone way too soon
A flower destined for greatness
That never had a chance to fully bloom
Stuck here with nothing but memories
They say "time heals all wounds"
But only you can fill this void in me
Time is something you can't buy or borrow
I'd give anything
To have one last moment with you
Even if I couldn't see tomorrow
A lot of things I wish we did
But we never had the chance
I guess life
Had its own change of plans
Every single day
I wish you never left me
I know it wasn't your choice
But the day you left this world
Whatever was left of my soul

You took the rest of me
I wish you would have never closed your eyes
And fallen asleep
Every day I keep reliving this nightmare
Wishing you'd call out my name
So I could wake up in peace
And this all could be just a dream

Grief

You came to me so suddenly
That I didn't know how to deal
So I buried you
With everything inside of me
Until life didn't feel real
On cloud 9, always on a high
Life felt so good
Living a lie in the sky
Running away from myself
The world felt so clear to me
When I couldn't see the truth
I was afraid to let you be
What you needed to be
Reality became too much for me
So I liberated myself
By numbing my feelings
I had every vice at my disposal
I found peace and solitude
In my destructive healing
Until the moment came
I couldn't keep up this façade
The high wore off
All of my enablers were gone
Now I was forced to face the reality
That tortured my mind
The place I've been dying to escape
For all this time

There's no magic potion
No pain pill for this relief
I welcome you with open arms
No more running away from my grief

Invisible Monster

You've plagued my mind
For my entire life
Creeping in the shadows
Coming out at the most inconvenient times
You see the smile on my face
But can't see the pain in my eyes
At war daily with myself
I'm slowly drowning within myself
I try to talk myself out of it
I try my best to make it make sense
But everything is a blur
I'm falling so far down off the deep end
I'm stranded, trapped and entangled
Inside this corroding body
My once strong, stable mind
Has now become mutilated and mangled
Peace no longer resides here
I'm a host of insecurities and fear
There's no notion of self
There's no notion of home
You've been here all my life
Still I always feel so alone

Peer Inside

Dying
To make sense of my confusion
Desperate
To find a reality in this illusion
Trying
To clear my mind of irrational delusion
Searching
For my joy that resides in my chaos
Coming to terms with this bed I've made
That I find hard to sleep in at night
Longing for a place I call home
In this endless space of my mind
Feeling lost and alone
Seeking validation at my wake
And peace of mind when I go to sleep at night
Haunted and burdened
By my own detrimental thoughts & anxieties
Where can I find the sanity in me?
Take me back, to when times were simple
Love was just a phenomenon and real life didn't
exist
Where pain was a scraped knee
Tears were a result of being an innocent spoiled
child
Take me back to the days I longed for
And the nights that didn't terrorize my dreams

Little Ole Me

It's all so vague
So cloudy
But some things I can't forget
No matter how bad I want to
Buried so deep in my mind
Yet the leftover trauma
Isn't hard to find
I tell myself maybe it's all in my head
Maybe it's just made up
Maybe you didn't really do that
Maybe you didn't really say that
Maybe you didn't really touch me like that
Maybe you didn't take advantage of my
innocence
You knew I wouldn't say a word
You knew I didn't know any better
You used to tell me
You couldn't wait until I was older
So you could really have your way with me
This was life
This was home
This is what I had come to know
At the tender age of 7 years old
What it was like to be mishandled
By someone who I trusted
Was someone whom trusted my ignorance and
fear
You're gone out of my life now
Yet the putrid taste of you
Still lingers in my senses

Trying to come to my senses
As you left me with scars that are endless
But you told that little girl it was okay
So that little girl kept quiet
Shattered, in deadly silence
These memories
Haven't died yet
Terrified to speak
In fear of choking on my own words
Sometimes you still have a hold on me
I replay your unwanted touch in my dreams
Then I wake up and face reality
Time still stings
Life still burns
Sometimes I'm still stuck
Sometimes I'm still that little girl
Even as time still turns

Happy Birthday

One sip away
From you crossing the line
You promised me
That everything was fine
When I knew deep down
You weren't in your right mind
Claimed to be my friend
But look at what you did
To avoid blame at all cost
Telling me this was all my fault
You didn't have the right
But I guess you didn't need it
You just pressured me until I said "yes"
Then you went in for the kill
Haunted
By this unforgettable nightmare
Trying to press delete
But it just keeps rewinding instead
Out of control
Out of my mind
I can't stop these flashbacks
I can't call them memories
Because my mind is not fond of these
These thoughts that rage
When I close my eyes to go to sleep
Your bone chilling aura
That sought out to take ahold of me

And make me its prey
Your touch still echoes on my skin
A night forever embedded in my mind
By the way
Thanks for the birthday memories

Blame

"It's your fault"
"You shouldn't have dressed that way"
"You lead him on, so you deserved it"
"You asked for it, so you can't complain"
"You didn't say no, so you wanted it"

That's what they tell you, isn't it?
Those are the words that echo in your mind
From people who could never know or
understand
They can't even begin to comprehend the horror,
trauma, guilt, disgust
That comes along with sexual abuse
No one takes that into account
No one takes into consideration
How violated you feel
But it's somehow "your" fault
No one holds them accountable
For taking something that doesn't belong to
them
Your security, sanity, peace of mind, pride, self-
worth and dignity
Are snatched right from underneath your feet
But you "know better" than to say anything
Because if you do
No one's going to believe you anyway
At least that's what they say, to keep you quiet
But don't let them silence you

You didn't ask for this and you sure as hell don't
deserve this!
Be bold, be brave, be courageous & fight!
Be a hero for yourself
And those who are afraid to speak up for
themselves
You didn't deserve this
But you do deserve happiness and peace of
mind
You are worthy of love and protection
There is a light at the end of the tunnel
So hold your head high
March forward in all of your glory
Take back your power
That rightfully belongs to you

Broken Promises

I made a promise to myself
That this wouldn't happen again
I wouldn't be like that little girl
Who let people take advantage of her
Who let people silence her
I made a promise to myself
That this wouldn't happen again
That I wouldn't let the world dim my shine
I wouldn't be like that little girl
Who was petrified to speak her mind
I made a promise to myself
That this wouldn't happen again
I wouldn't let them break me
I wouldn't let them hurt me
I wouldn't let them near me
I wouldn't let them touch me
I made a promise to myself
Not to let predators prey on me
And to seek help for these demons I keep
I made a promise to myself
To give my mother her stone for her resting
place
Since it's the final thing I could offer her
I made a promise to myself
To not be hardened by this cold hearted, vile
world
Only to find myself
Curled up on the floor
Like that helpless little girl
That I never wanted to see or be again

I made countless promises to myself
But they're all broken
I never fulfilled them
I gave up hope in me
Still trying to find
The pieces to my broken peace

Scarlet Letter

It's a bloody mess
I think it's finally time
That we put this love to rest
My heart ripped wide open
I fought to the death of me
Even though I knew better
Written with the blood of love
Was your name over my heart
Signed by the love of a lifetime
On this scarlet letter

Detached

I unpack the memories
Every time you make love to me
Plagued by the thought
Of the past repeating itself
Vulnerability leaves me open
To the exposure of the truth
I shun out all emotion
And erase it from my mind
Peering through the shadows
Trying to find the old me, I left behind
Covered in anxiety
Crippled with loneliness
Knowing if I push everyone away
No one can hurt me
A flower can't grow without rain
But too much rain leads to overflow
What a constant overload
Of feeling so alone
Misunderstood
But not wanting to be understood
Because if you understood me
That means you'll know me
And if you know me
That means you know how to hurt me
Paranoia
Leaves me watching my back
Making sure to keep my heart

Safe from attack
I can't let you get too close
So I make sure to stay emotionally detached
Keep you at arm's length
Even though I wish I had arms to hold me
Yearning for love
But fearing love would disown me
I can't let myself get too close
Because if I do, I'll fall in love
And I'm scared for you to love me

Spilled Milk

Sitting at the kitchen table
Reminiscing on every single breakfast
That we shared over the past 2 years
Crying over spilled milk
Only the milk consisted of
The love, time and effort
That went unreciprocated
Glass half full
With regret and questions
My love and mind
Spilled and splattered
All across the table
Dripping onto the floor
Falling
At a millennium a second
I patiently waited
For an eternity
For you to love me
But you took me for granted
You couldn't even wipe up
The spilled milk off the floor

Empty Cup

I filled you with love
You left me empty
Waiting to be fulfilled
I gave you my life
While you left me for dead
A puddle of memories and love
Made from my never ending streams of tears
At a crossroad with love
Not knowing
Whether to go with my heart or mind
Constantly pouring myself
Into a bottomless pit of self-destruction
Constantly being drained
Of my good love and giving heart
Constantly giving and giving
With getting little to nothing in return
I gave you all my love
You gave me nothing
But false hope and heartache
Exhausted from this constant back and forth
Letting go and holding on
Bleeding
Dying to let go
Why is it so hard to let go?
Even of the thing that's killing you?
I gave you my heart
Filled you with life

While you left me empty
Waiting to be fulfilled

Disposable

Lost in the crowd
I'm looking for you
But you're too far to see
All I see are strangers around me
Seems like you're life times ahead of me
You only look back for a second
In a glimpse
You've faded like a distant shadow
Trying to keep up
But you keep knocking me down
Am I just a burden
That weighs you down?
Am I just a waste
That's so easily disposable?
You drift away from me slowly
Taking my heart and my love with you
I was the memory
You forgot to remember

Faded

The flame starts to die down
The light starts to flicker
Your glow grows dimmer
Shots become bottles
Sleepless nights
Turn into mornings we wish never came
Where did we go
We go lost
Wandering around
Trying to find
What was right in front of us
The song is over
The melody ended
We stopped dancing a long time ago
Just the same old memories on repeat
Lying with a stranger every night
In a bed of lukewarm love
Where did you go
You got lost
Wandering around
Searching for the fire that you blew out
While I stood around
Waiting to ignite your heart
One last time

Love Drought

It only gets harder
The longer you hold on
Fighting your way
Through the everlasting storm
Confused and anxious
Trying so desperately to stay strong
But there's a crack in the vault
Right at the entrance of the heart
Battling all of the past trauma and scars
Day in, day out
You try to make sense of it all
But the ground isn't stable
So all you do is fail
Every time you fall
Get back up to pick up the pieces
So you peek through the creases
Searching for any way out
From constant ridicule and doubt
Unfortunately you can't escape
In their heart, lies a love drought

One Day

One day
You'll stumble upon the rain
That fell from my heart
The night I cried my soul away
One day your feet will pace
Those silent hallways
Where our laughs would echo for hours
One day you'll lay your head
On the oakwood floor
In front of the fireplace
Where we made love every night
And drown into the memory of my tender touch
One day you'll look into the eyes
Of the woman you love
And memories of me will flood your mind
One day you'll gaze into the sunrise
And reminisce of those happier times
One day you'll look into the mirror
And see my face staring back at you
On a warm summer night
The moonlight will shine upon you
Only to cast the shadow of an old flame
One day you'll think of me
By then I'll only be a distant memory

Rewind

Let's uncross that line
Press reset
Go back in time
When we were just two strangers
Who never met
Take back the memories
I long to forget
Freeze frame in time
Before I fell for it all
When our hearts would slow dance
When you made love to me
When your sweet words would touch my heart
Now they barely hit my ears
Your lips used to send shivers down my spine
Now when we kiss, I don't even feel you
Your love has left the room
Leaving me cold and disenchanted
My heart mangled and tattered
The memories won't fade away
So I press replay every day
Each time I pray
You'll piece me back together again

The Girl Who Used to Love You

I want to be like her
The girl who used to love you
Who thought she needed you
But somehow deleted you
I envy her
The girl who used to love you
Because she used to be in my shoes
Now she's moved passed you
And found someone new
She loved you once
And fell out of love with you
Somehow, I fell in love with you
And I got stuck
Now I feel like I can't get out
My heart nailed to the palm of your hand
Praying that you don't pulverize it
I never thought I'd be that girl
The one who knew better
But didn't do better
The girl who let her heart lead the way
Instead of letting common sense
Be my friend
But I fell in love
And sometimes love doesn't go as planned

Vices

Some people drink it away
Some people sex it away
Some people drug it away
Some people starve it away
Some people puke it away
Some people cut it away
Some people write it away
Some people smoke it away
Some people sing it away
Some people numb it away
Some people cry it away
Some people laugh it away
Some people dance it away
Some people draw it away
Some people erase themselves completely
We all have our vices
That help us deal with the pain

Chapter 2
Dreamland

"The fog is so thick
4:44 AM
I let my soul drift"

Goodnight

4:44 AM
I let my soul drift
The fog is so thick
I can barely see the street lights
Fresh out the shower
Nestled underneath a million blankets
Serenity encapsulates me
Eyes peering
Into the frosty early morning
Heart wide open
Embracing the November breeze
Anxiously awaiting sunrise
As the moon winds down
Only to go hiding behind the fog
Relaxation music meddling in the background
Mind is heavy with anxiety
But I'll leave my worries for the morning
Goodnight darkness
I'll see you tomorrow at sunset

Meet Me in My Dreams

Meet me in my dreams
Where reality cease to exist
Digging for gold
Looking for priceless dreams you sold
Color you pretty
Won't you paint this fantasy with me
Laughs cackle in the wind
Memories run wild
Only to be left behind
Ocean waves
Sunset beach
Love is life's greatest fruit
Sweet as a peach
Daydreaming into the sunset
Don't worry we're not done yet
Stars trickle out of the sky
The moon roars at the peak of night
Moonlight kisses our skin
Not looking for a way out
Of this love ridden sin
Footprints embedded in the sand
Only to be washed up at the shore
Heart echoes in the waves of love
Starry eyes, sandy skin
Kiss me in the ocean
Dive into my soul
Naked and unafraid
We make love
On crystals of pink sand
Deeper we sink

The deeper we fall
The deeper we bury life
Underneath it all
We create our own truths
Forever stuck
In this bed of passion and lust, we lie
Crashing hard from this love high
Catch me in your gentle breeze
Just promise me every night
You'll meet me in my dreams

Dreamy Hills

Falling down
From these dreamy hills
Dying for the thrill
Dying for a love that kills
My insecurities
And loves every part of me
The good
The bad
The beautiful
The ugly
A love that fulfills my needs
A love that supersedes
Anything I could ever dream
A love
That wraps me in its wings
And makes my heart sing
Magical melodies
From the bottom of my heart
To the very top
Of those dreamy hills

Anticipation

Cherry blossom petals
Fiery red sky
As the sun winds down
Rose blushed skin
Silky, freshly bathed hair
Eyes green as emerald
Your soft sweet scent
Races in the evening wind
My heart awaits your arrival
As your feet hurry
Into the moonless night
Shooting stars illuminate
Your eager eyes
As they gaze upon mine
Your arms caress my body
With such love, delicacy and gentleness
My body quickly melts
Into the mold of your tender soul
Silently, lovingly and sweetly
Your heart whispers the melody of love
Quietly, patiently and intently
My heart anxiously listens to its story
Burning with an appetite for love
Lusting for a taste of bliss
Your sacred secret of love
I unlock with a kiss

Field of Lilies

The moon stands
Not a cloud in sight
Not a star within its reach
The moon stands
At its highest peak
Glowing in the dark
Kissing everything
Beneath its feet
Here we are
You and me
Gazing at its beauty
While we listen to it speak
These flowers are my favorite
They shine the best at night
White velvet lilies
That glow in the dark
And light up
Our love stricken hearts
Can we just stay here
Forever
Falling in love
In this endless field of lilies

<u>An Endless Forever</u>
Strobe lights
Starry skies
Cotton candy dreams
Sweet as honey
Love
Strong as steel
Imagination running wild
Innocence of a child
Contagious smiles
Pretty hazel eyes
Love stained lips
Stain fingertips
Secrets
Whisper in the wind
Laughs travel
Deep to the ocean floor
Dreams
Spread across the horizon
The sun sets
While the night rises
Moon kissed fields
Flowers and fireflies
Kissing underneath the stars
Pass the midnight hour
Legs in a hurry
To reach the love of a lifetime
Rain showers
That bring about florescent rainbows
Angels
Become memories buried in the snow

Naive hearts
That glow in the dark
Star gazing
Into the eyes of forever

Awakening of Dawn

The moon is moving at a faster pace tonight
Running from the shadows
Trying to hide its light within the stars
Bright as day
The light that casts shadows in the night
A glow so mesmerizing
It's almost impossible
Not to be caught in a trance
The sun drowns into the horizon
To wake the moon from its slumber
Ever so slowly
The tides of the night sky shifts
And the stars make way
For God's glorious creation
So silent, so still, so hypnotizing
So obscure
Yet wonderous and fascinating
Nature moves at its calling
Out comes the creatures of the nocturnal realm
There goes the scattered fragments of sunlight
For dawn has fallen upon us
And all that awaits
Is the reality of life that comes at morning

Chapter 3
Sex, Love & Lust

"A flame froze in time. Right where I left you"

37 Mornings

See you in 37 mornings
37 mornings
Till I see your face
You're my favorite rose
In this garden of love
37 mornings
Till you become mine
My sunrise and sunshine
36 nights
Till I become whole
36 nights
Till I touch your soul
36 days
36 sunrises
36 sunsets
36 full moons
36 new moons
Same me
Same you
See you in 37 mornings
Morning seems so far away
Time stops
As the days waste away
My love
Good morning
My love
The countdown is over
Our time apart is up
My sunrise
My sunshine

My favorite rose
In this love we've created
My love
Good morning, my love

Comfortably Vulnerable

I see golden rays
Shine across your face
As I kiss you awake
You open your eyes and grin
Gazing into my eyes
We lay in bed
Drifting into another space
Sun kissed lips
Waking up in a daze
Your arms around my waist
Face to face, skin to skin
So comfortably vulnerable
In our own little world we're in

Everything's Different

Everything's different
When you're in love
The shade of black in your eyes disappears
The fire slowly starts to glimmer & shine
That jaded and bitter heart of yours
Grows and glows with faith and hope
Your impenetrable exterior
Ever so carefully starts to soften and fade away
Kissing isn't the same
You can feel the passion with every sweet taste
Your hands are no longer frozen and lifeless
Your heartbeat pounds through your fingertips
There's no longer an ominous aura in your
presence
Your heart beams from head to toe
Sex isn't mechanical and emotionless
There's passion, comfortability and love making
The air is much lighter
The load isn't as heavy and burdensome
Life is just a little bit easier
Nights aren't as lonely
Mornings now come with eagerness
As you await love's awakening from sleep
Everything's different
When you're in love

Love

Everyone searches for it
Yet very few find it

Right in front of your eyes
Yet you don't see it

Right at the tips of your fingers
Yet you're still unable to touch it

Lost and found
Again and again, have I given up on it

It makes you laugh and cry
They say it's the best thing in the world

Never in my life
Have I felt so happy because of this

This one thing
I just can't resist

I've tried over and over
To keep this under control

But when it comes to you, my love
My heart has no restrictions

Romance

Candlelight dinner
Homemade love
Hearts slow dancing
In front of the fireplace
Tender kisses
Heartfelt love confessions
Sensual without sexual
Sacred love making
But the only thing you've touched
Is my curious mind
Breathtaking secrets
Only to be revealed
By our love anxious bodies
Screaming hot
Burning passion
Yet we don't allow it to overwhelm us
In the heat of the night
Stars plummet from the sky
Never ending
As our fire blazes forever

Intimacy

Intimate sessions
Without taking our clothes off
Turn on your mind
Let me see what goes off
You made love to me
Without even touching my body
Vibrations from your lips
Shook something inside me
My lips feel ice cold
While patiently waiting for yours
They don't feel right naked
Unless they're covered in yours
You're nothing short of fascination
Sex beyond my wildest imagination
More than anything I've ever expected
You've fallen for me
Just accept it

Love That Transcends Time

It all happened in an instant
Between time and space
There was no distance

A spark that grew into a flame
In that very moment
I never saw love the same

One thing lead to another
Feelings had blossomed
And we fell in love with each other

Not a moment was taken for granted
As if time itself stood still
Frozen, our hearts stood stranded

Let's explore love without boundaries
Somewhere in this cold hard world
Your lost heart found me

Looking at you with nothing to say
A serenity that speaks volumes
I can feel your love, from galaxies away

Captivated by your essence
In your eyes behold the girl
Who comes alive in your presence

Tender Innocence

Lying in bed
Wide awake
Can't seem to fall asleep
Wondering what you're dreaming about
Sleeping right next to me
Silly little smirk on your face
A smile, I pray
That my mind will never erase
Window wide open
Your hair is singing in the breeze
Freshly bathed
Your subtle scent
Puts my heart at ease
Dying to snuggle next to you
But I'm too afraid to wake you
Yet somehow
I finagle myself underneath your arm
Your hair tickles my nose
I'm only breaths away
From those tender, sweet lips
How they seem so inviting
But I'm too shy to taste you

First Time

I've never done this before
Still, my body welcomes you
The excruciating excitement
As you enter between my legs
My walls
Begin to crumble
Crushing everything in their path
But damn
It's never felt so good
The look in your eyes
I can tell
You want to take me there
To a world of euphoria
As my senses heighten
My legs start convulsing
As my body
Allows you to take me higher
There goes all sense of control
As the levee breaks
And my divine femininity
Starts to unfold
The river gushes forth
Drenching you with love
Not a single drop
Went untasted

Tease

I tease you
And taste you
For just a quick second
The look of disappointment
On your face
That it was over and done too quickly
But the look in your eyes
Told me you wanted to tear me to shreds
I happily welcome
Your sexual destruction
Take control
Own It
Have me
Anyway you want it
Tie me up
Strap me down
Bite me
Tease me
Let your warm tongue
Make love to my clit
As my body becomes engorged
Ready to explode
At any given lick
Choke me
Till I'm almost out of breath
Drink all of my juices
Till there's nothing left

Give it to me
Till I can't take anymore
Make me beg on my knees
Baby
Do as you please
Unfortunately now
The fun has come to an end
Too bad it's time to wake up
Damn what a beautiful dream
If only
My mind wasn't such a tease

Satin Sheets

Woke up at 7 AM
Last night's sin
Still feels fresh
To be honest
Your flavor
Tastes the best
What a hell of a night
Of sex excess
Don't remember much
We were pretty faded
Don't know what hit first
Being drunk off your love
Or being high off your sex
Started off in the bed
Ended up on the ground
Hit after hit
Round after round
Your face buried in the pillow
Just to keep the screaming down
Last thing I remember
Was me
Tasting between your legs
Gripping the sheets
Dripping in sweat
Leaving the satin sheets
Soaking wet
Love stains
All over the place
Fingernail scratches
All over my body

Bite marks
Embedded in my skin
Guess I felt so good
That you couldn't hold it in
Satin sheets
Made with love
Covered in sin

Taste of Sin

They told you to stay away
But you didn't listen
Now you've gotten a taste of my love
Something feels different

I got you hooked
It's so euphoric
Hypnotized by the vibe
You didn't even notice

A feeling that has you curious
Yet you're so delirious
It's an infection of lust and passion
Let's make this sin everlasting

So much heat and friction
You can't even catch your breath
Let the passion burn
Until we fade into ashes

Lost, trying to find your way to me
But your lips still remember the taste of me
So your tongue searches for me in the dark

Trapped inside this raging fire

Watch as the smoke rises
Captivated in this body high
We're mesmerized

Slow down
The fun hasn't even started yet
I haven't even touched your body
And you're already dripping in sweat

Sit back and relax
Watch my body but stay focused
Tension at an all-time high
Might cause an overdose

It's an adrenaline rush
Don't stop just yet
The water's getting deep
Make sure you hold your breath

My legs shake and my teeth chatter
I just want all of you
Harder, deeper and faster

So electric, sensual and erotic
I'll take you higher and higher
A place meant for the exotic

This taste of sin, let me pour it
Drink up, I hope you enjoy it

Fixation of You

Lust at first sight
Fire from the first touch
I didn't know your past
But your presence spoke to me
A smile forever engraved in my mind
A body my fingertips could never forget
With every touch I wanted you more
Despite the fact
You never once touched me back
My hands spoke to you
Though my lips never whispered a word
What a glow you have to you
Such a mesmerizing glow
A captivating glow
A dangerous glow
I couldn't help
But to be drawn into your mysteries
Wondering what was beyond this body
This sinfully beautiful body
Tall, dark, soft, gentle, quiet, soft spoken,
charismatic
I was so curious
To what lied deep within the exterior
The thoughts, triggers, emotions, passions and
sexual desires
That were hidden
Deep inside of you
But I don't know you
I'll never know you
I only know your shell

Your body
That sinfully beautiful body

Please

Please don't start
If you're not going to finish
Don't excite my body
Don't ignite my fire
If you're not going to let the chaos rage
Please don't touch me
If you're not going to taste me
Please don't tease me
If you're not going to relieve me
Of this pounding and unbearable
Sexual prison I'm in
Don't let me taste you
If I can't completely satisfy
My wet appetite
I need you
I crave you
I want you
To destroy me
In the best way possible
Please
Don't open the gates
Don't unleash the waterfall
If you're not ready to drown in me

Misunderstanding

It was those vicious eyes
That stripped me naked
And unveiled
Every nasty thing
I've dreamt of doing to you
Every time you'd look into my eyes
Or maybe
It was the way
You told me how good I felt
Every time I touched you
I love putting you to sleep
When it's all said and done
I love the way
You say my name
While you were grabbing her ass
Or someone else just finished having you
The sexual tension
That would knock the life out of me
Make me drip to the bone
And make me want you
That much more
Those succulent lips
That I yearned to taste
Every inch
Of my sex ridden skin
I love the way

You fuck me
When it's just you and I
All alone, in my mind
But maybe it was all in my head
Maybe you didn't want me
The way I desperately craved you
It must have been
A simple misunderstanding

Old Flame

You scream out to my body
I come running to you
When you come knocking on the door
Of the memories in my mind
I want to resist you
But I can't say no to you
My body is forever
A part of you
Raw and completely vulnerable
No protection
I dive in heart first
Body over matter
My mind overtakes my body
Nothing makes sense
Except the taste of your sin
Nothing makes sense
Except the vibrations of your skin
Searching for you in the dark
I don't want this to end
Too good to behold
Too deep to uncover
But I don't want to uncover
I want to stay wrapped up in you
Forever
Tossing and turning
Our souls fight
Only to ignite

In the heat of ecstasy
You filled me in all the right ways
You felt good in all the wrong ways
You still have my body in a chokehold
Even on my best days
Years with you
Can't be erased
By millenniums without you
You know my body
Better than I know my soul
I compare every touch to yours
But none of them measure up
You taste just as good
As the last time I had you
A flame frozen in time
Right where I left you

Chapter 4
Reflective

"Just because it doesn't hurt as bad. Doesn't mean it doesn't hurt at all"

You Remind Me of Home

You remind me of home
The broken hell where I come from
A place I was tolerated
Put up with and put down
Where instability and uncertainty resided
A place of constant changing faces
Filled with abandonment, abuse & neglect
You remind me of home
Full of screaming, cussing, crying and beatings
Never feeling safe & having no one to lean on
One wrong mistake, one accidental slip up
Would bring a whirlwind of everlasting hell
You remind me of pain
You remind me of trauma
You remind me of fear
I remind you of home
A place you never want to visit again

You Can't Hurt Me
"You can't hurt me, no one can hurt me"

Those were the lies I told myself
Repeatedly for years after my mom died
So much that I started to believe them myself
It was my number 1 go to defense mechanism
I'd use if someone hurt me
I figured I lost my mom
So how could anything hurt me like losing her?
I built up a wall
To protect and guard myself
But in all actuality
I protected myself, due to fear
Fear of what could possibly hurt me
So, I'd walk around acting tough
To hide the agonizing pain I was going through
Sad to say
It was all a façade
Some play the role better than others
But sooner or later
Pain unravels itself
In one way or another
Pain is still pain
No matter the capacity
Just because it doesn't hurt as bad
Doesn't mean it doesn't hurt at all

Human

I usually hide it pretty well
I usually deal with it pretty well
For whatever reason
I feel this need to be constantly strong or okay
Like I have my life and emotions together
All the time
Sometimes I forget I'm human
A human with a past
A woman with a story to tell
Life old wounds that still need healing
A lot of demons that still need facing
And a life so painfully beautiful
That I get so lost in the pain
That I forget the beauty
A lot of trauma that I've encountered
A lot of secrets that sometimes still haunt me
So I just deal by numbing the pain and pushing
through
But at night is when it gets real
That's when the truth comes out
Just me and the darkness that resides in me
And the demons that I keep buried deep
Because I don't know how to manage them or
face them
So I ignore them
Until they make me acknowledge them
I'm running from myself

My worries
My insecurities and weaknesses
Thinking
I can escape it all
Sometimes I forget I'm only human

Change of Rules

I thought I was ready for love
Until love came before me
Then I got scared and ran away
How dare you deny me
Of everything I'm used to
And give me everything I've ever wanted?
You told me to take pride in myself
That I'm more than just a vessel for pleasure
That I'm made of a body of love
What kind of a man are you?
This is too good to be true
Who are you to come along
And show me what love is?
Who are you to come along
And take your time with me?
Who are you to come along
And really want to get to know me?
You're all I've ever wanted
And everything I never knew I needed
I thought I was ready for love
Until I realize I had to love myself first
Before I could accept love from a man

Unraveled

Seeing your roots
Helps me understand how you grow
Unlocking your mind
Helps me understand the way you perceive life
I always thought I knew you
But oh what a difference there is
In simply knowing
And deeply understanding
Your mannerism & characteristics
Who you are as a man
Your past
Paves the path to your present
But I only scratched the surface
I never took the time to dig deep
Then you started to unravel
You let me strip back the layers
Even though it was unbearable for you at times
You let me into your world, existence and being
You lifted the veil that covered your heart
And revealed to me the darkness
That was dormant underneath
Tangled within the darkness
Were pieces of love, hope, wanting and faith
Though scattered and fragmented
It was still possible to bring them together
Slowly the darkness started to corrode
There I saw your heart and all of its essence

You were no longer afraid to bare your soul to
me
And I was no longer afraid to love you

Teach Me

I thought I knew it all
The ins and outs of love
I swore I knew it all
There's only one way to love
Straight & narrow
No diverting or obstacles
To get in my way of love
Till I stumbled upon a broken man
One with many scars
And a traumatic upbringing
Who turned my world upside down
And confused everything
That once made sense
In my simple minded mind
So much damage, so much baggage
And here I am left with the broken pieces
Not sure if I'm ready to unpack yet
I found you in the midst of finding myself
Didn't think I needed a man
But truth be told, I did
Not to love me
But to show me how to love
Show me how to build from the ground up
Baby steps
That resulted in leaps and bounds
Unconditionally, patiently, gently and kindly
Is how I learned to love you

While I was also learning to love myself
You've taught me the ins and outs
That I truly knew nothing about
You taught me how to love
Someone who's never been loved

Sometimes

Sometimes I want to be lost in the dark
Sometimes I want to be found in the light
Sometimes I want to give up
Other times I want to put up a fight
Sometimes I feel ugly
Sometimes I feel beautiful
Sometimes I want something deep
Sometimes I want something superficial
Sometimes I want to laugh
Sometimes I break down and cry
Sometimes I'm happy
Other times I'm sad and don't know why
Sometimes I'm carefree
Other times I'm anxious
Sometimes I want to be known
Other times I want to remain nameless
Sometimes I wish it was fake
Sometimes I want it to be real
Sometimes the pain is too much to feel
Sometimes I feel smart
Sometimes I feel dumb
Sometimes I feel everything
But most times I feel numb
Sometimes I'm my own best friend
Most times I'm my own worst enemy
Sometimes I feel on top of the world

Other times
I wonder if I still have the strength left in me
Sometimes I want love
Sometimes I want to be alone forever
Sometimes I feel like my life's falling apart
Sometimes I think I have it all together
Sometimes I'm brave
Sometimes I live in fear
Sometimes I smile
Just to hide the countless tears
Sometimes I feel stuck to the ground
Sometimes I feel I can reach the sky
Sometimes I wish I had somewhere to run
So I could cast reality aside

Self-Destruction

You were the darkness
That would wrap its arms around me
To keep me warm
You were my hell on earth
Who made sense of all of my storms
You were the black hole
That I couldn't wait to get lost in
The quicksand
I could always sink in
The pain
I never knew I needed
The disappointment
I always believed in
The warning
I never took heed in
The perfect love
That left me bleeding
The blind
I followed the lead in
Destructive in every possible way
Yet here I am
Staring in the mirror
Falling more in love with you
Every single day

Dear Me

I know we've been at war for quite some time
I know I've made you feel so out of place
Inside your own mind
We've never been friends
Not even the distant kind
You've tried so hard
To follow in the right footsteps
But that path
Has led us to much anguish and regret
I've come to accept you
Still learning to love you
Remembering to never neglect you
Even if the world somehow forgets you
I know I've let you down
A million and one, too many times
I'm sorry
For leaving you on the ground
I'm sorry
I'm finally falling in love with you now
I'm sorry
For abandoning you for all of those years
I know
You're still healing childhood wounds and
conquering fears
Please stop telling yourself you're not good
enough
Stop giving yourself to people who don't

deserve you
You've given enough
Stop looking for validation in others
Stop begging for love
Stop telling yourself you're asking for too much
It's okay to not be okay
It's okay to ask for help
I promise you
It's okay to love yourself

Destiny

We were destined to meet
Were we destined to fall in love?
Was I destined to fall and break?
Were you destined to break me?
Or did you simply forsake me?
Was I destined to love you?
Were you destined to leave me?
Were our worlds destined to collide?
Were we destined to catch fire?
Were our hearts meant to run wild?
Was my heart made for a lifetime?
Was my heart destined to be blind?
Is your heart destined to be mine?
Here we are
You and me
I am you
You are me
Am I destined to break free?
Or are you destined to eliminate me?

Guilty

I'm sorry I left you
In your dire time of need
I wanted to get through to you
Unfortunately
I couldn't succeed
I wanted you to need me
But you only wanted pain and misery
I felt guilty for leaving
But I had to keep my sanity
I'm so sorry
I hope you understand
Your insanity
Was causing me anxiety
I tried to fight for you
But I lost the fight in me
It tore me up inside
Knowing there was no way out
Of your own misery
Stuck in the same space
While your life was falling out of place
I tried keeping it all together
But I couldn't keep up the pace
Depression and abuse
Became your usual
To you a healthy and happy life
Was so unusual
I was dying to keep you alive

But we were drowning together
So I had to let go
The storm I could no longer weather
But now you're stronger
Stronger than you've ever been before
I hope one day you find it
The peace you've been dying for

You

Who are you
When it's just you
Left alone
With all of your fears and anxieties?
When the roaring noise
Suddenly goes quiet?
Who are you
When you look in the mirror
And you can't even recognize yourself?
Who are you
Outside of this world's life?
Who are you
Behind the scenes
When your "perfect world"
Is falling apart
And your mind is ripping at its seams?
Who are you
Outside of your dreams
When reality hits you in the face
And you have to figure out
What "living" really means?
Who were you
Before the world traumatized you
Made you change yourself
Because you were petrified of being an outcast
Who are you
Inside your own body

Inside your own mind
When it's just you
All alone
With all of your anxieties and fears
That keep you warm?

Chapter 5
Hope & Breakthrough

"Sometimes we don't recognize the blessings. Until we're out of the storm"

Free My Soul

A caged bird imprisoned
Behind these silent walls
My soul, on the brink of extinction
My faith, has crumbled beneath it all
I'm trapped within darkness
Please help me escape
My time for freedom is growing near
I can no longer wait
Lift my head to the sky
Ready to see the light
Ready to spread my wings
Ready to witness the forsaken things
Allow your love
To set the world free
Take my hand
Come fly with me
I need to break free from this mold
Life has me in a choke hold
Just God please
Free my soul

God's Timing

Wading
In these troublesome waters
Trying my best
To stay afloat
Praying to God
He won't let me drift away
I should know better
I should have more faith
God, oh God
I know
You created me to survive
You created me to thrive
You created me to live
You'd never leave me to drown
And if I were to go under
You're never too far away
To pull me back up for air
Even in the deepest oceans
Even in my darkest hours
I can see your pure and perfect light
Guiding this rugged path of mine
You've never forsaken me
Forgive me
For I have forsaken myself
I've let the darkness take ahold of me
I let temptation and imperfection
Rob me of your precious gifts

I've allowed fleshly desires
To cloud my judgment
And leave me in the trenches
The devil has seeped into my mind
Bleeding out false lies
Making me believe
That I could never be loved by you again
But all in your timing
Will you bring me forth
From this bitter cold and darkness
All in your timing
Will you quiet the noise and chatter
That the devil speaks upon your holy name
God, my God
Thank you for forgiving me
Never forsaking me
Even though I strayed
From your righteous path

All I Need

God love me
Through all the turbulence and pain
God hold me
When I feel weak in my knees
When I can't even stand
God keep me close
Because sometimes I wander down the wrong
path
Sometimes I wander into the darkness
God guide me
Because I feel so lost in my heart and soul
God find me
Because I feel like I'm losing myself
I think I've lost my mind
God calm my heart
I'm filled with so much anxiety and fear
God shower me
With your undying love
Because I've lost all sense of love
I feel so abandoned by love
I feel so abandoned by myself
And those who claim to love me
God spare me
I feel like I'm dying
God give me life
Give me air to breathe
I feel like I'm suffocating
Inside my worry and mistakes
Please take my hand
I'm holding on for dear life

Desperately trying not to drown
The walls are caving
The waves are crashing
The devil is out to kill my soul
He's out to demolish my hope
God raise me up
From this sunken place
From this black whole
Let me lean on you
Let me love you
Let me trust in you
Let me hope in you
Please be my stronghold
Be my shelter
Be my rock
Be the only evidence of perfection
In this imperfect and tarnished world

You Saved Me

From death and destruction
Through you I was rescued
When the shadows and darkness came
You were my refuge
God really blessed me
When he gave me you
All the chaos and pain
You've seen me through
In ups and downs
You've been my go to
From everything I let go
To everything I held inside
My tears and fears
You've cast aside
Emotional rollercoasters
You were always down to ride
Egotistical or low
You banished my pride
When I wanted to fall to pieces
Together, you kept me
And when I wanted to give up on myself
You never left me
Opened my eyes to the truth
To which I was blind
Thank God
You saved me

Light at the End of the Tunnel

People think they know what it's like, to live in darkness. Not physical darkness, but emotional darkness. Constant turmoil, day in and day out, that you never speak of. Fake smiles and pretty eyes, that cover up daily depression and anxiety.

What's it like to live inside your own mind, where no one can see what goes on? What's it like to be trapped behind a wall, that not even you can break down? What's it like not being able to see that light at the end of the tunnel? What if there is no light? What if there is no way out? What if there is no such thing as happiness? What if there is no such thing as tomorrow? What if today was the last day you would see darkness? What if the load is too overbearing? What if the pressure is too heavy? What if you couldn't bear one more second of life?

That's what it's like living with depression, anxiety and suicidal thoughts. But people deem mental illness as a joke or even not real.

"It's all in your head"

"Just get over it"

"Just be happy"

"Just take some pills, you'll be fine"

"It's just a phase you'll be okay eventually"

That's what they **ALL** say because they're ignorant or simply don't want to acknowledge that suicide and depression are real life issues that millions of people suffer from **EVERY SINGLE DAY**!

But what if I told you there is a way out. You don't have to be trapped; you can break down those walls. There **IS** a light at the end of the tunnel. You **CAN** see tomorrow. You **DON'T** have to carry the load alone.

There are people who love you and want you to live, thrive, love and be loved. You're so much more than you make yourself out to be. You're worthy of everything you've ever wanted, and you deserve all the love in the world. You must love and accept yourself but know that the world doesn't need to love you in order for you to be amazing. The world doesn't define who you are as a person or your self-worth/value, **ONLY YOU CAN DEFINE YOU**!

Don't give others the power of controlling your life. Take control of your happiness, your life, your mental and physical health. Don't be ashamed to speak out and to speak up because you need to be heard, you **DESERVE** to be heard. I promise the pain is only temporary. Keep fighting, please don't give up.

You deserve happiness

You deserve to live....

Pray for Us All

Hey you
You with the broken heart
It'll take some time
But the pieces will come back together
To the lover
Who's loved too hard
But has never been loved in return
There's someone out there
Who'll cherish your golden heart
To the lonely and socially awkward
Don't worry
You'll find your crowd
To the child, who is now an adult
You've had to navigate this world on your own
No more worrying
You'll find your way home
To life and to love
To the one who's given themselves
To any man or woman
Because they felt "something is better than
nothing"
Who led a life of sexual promiscuity
Because you felt you weren't worth anything
else
I promise you
You're worth so much more
Than a life of being used
To the person
Who pursued their dreams over money
Just know it'll pay off in more ways

106

Than you could only imagine
To the child who grew up
Knowing only neglect and abuse
I get it, you don't know how to love
Or how to receive love
But it's never too late to learn
For love is never too late
To the girl who looks at a man
For the things her absent father never gave her
There's so much more validation to you
Than a man who is unable to love you
You must love yourself first
In order to understand
To the woman
Who's "only pretty for a big girl"
Beauty goes as deep as you allow it to
To the single mom, single dad
Who's desperately trying to make every penny
last
Your efforts don't go unnoticed, stay focused
To you with the troubled past
Who gives everything, yet never asks
You'll find people who appreciate you
To the delicate man or woman
Whose heart is so soft to the touch
Don't let this cold world harden you
To the person who wants their world to end
Because the weight of the world is too heavy
You don't have to carry the load alone
To the adult
Who was sexually abused as a child

Forgive them, forgive yourself
For you deserve to heal in peace

Blue Ocean Dreams

Here comes the tidal waves
My heart's not safe
Frozen in fear I stand
Better brace for impact
But nothing
Could hold your love back
The waves came crashing down
Your love came rushing through
Bombarding the entirety
Of my vulnerable being
Caught off guard
My anxious and dubious heart
Frantically searching for the surface
In dire need of air
Thankfully
My efforts were futile
I was being dragged down
Deep down into your heart
Where peace and love resides
Love droplets
Ripple effects
The waves calm and soothe me
I sink deeper
While my worries and troubles
Wash away
God!
That's what your love does to me

It cleanses me
Purifies my soul
Deeper, I sink
Drowning inside
Your blue ocean dreams

Lean on Him

Sometimes we don't recognize the blessings
Until we're out of the storm
Though your body may be tired
And your soul may be worn
When you're feeling cold and lonely
He is there to guide you and keep you warm
Broken down, feet dragging on the ground
When you're full of doubt
And you start losing sight of your hope
Looking for a helping hand
Not sure on how to cope
When you're feeling lost at sea
Suffocating from anxiety and you can't breathe
There's hope where the sun and skyline meet
God is just waiting for you to open your eyes
and see
Just beyond the horizon
Is a new day, new light, new love
That awaits you to find your joy
Reach out to him
He's always there to pull you back up
No matter how far you think you've fallen

Thank You God

I remember
Begging you
Not to wake me from my sleep
Now I thank you
For letting me live my dreams
The world can feel so heavy
But you make the load light
You are the truth
You are the way
You are the light
Thank you God
For all that you've given me
For you see the beauty in me
That sometimes I cannot see
You gently reprove me
While guiding me in the right direction
You see the real me
Beyond all my imperfection
Thank you God
For your undeserving kindness and patience
Thank you
For taking me by the hand
And leading me to your everlasting love

ACKNOWLEDGEMENTS
First and foremost I have to thank God for giving me the gift of writing.
The gift to move and touch people's hearts in ways I never knew I could.

Kristin, what a beautiful masterpiece we've created. I knew deep in my heart you were the right woman to do this with & I don't regret my decision. It was a rough start, but we pushed through together and I can't thank you enough. Your attention to detail, time, patience, love, heart & soul that you put into this is beyond this world. Our friendship is something I'll cherish forever & I'm beyond ecstatic to create more together. Thank you for everything.

To my dad who's always been so supportive of my writing from the first poem he ever read of mine, I can't thank you enough. You've always encouraged me to give it my all no matter what. We've come a long way and I love you to death.

To all of my friends who've seen my writing evolve from middle school until now and still love these pieces of art that I create, your love never goes unnoticed. I can never thank you guys enough for encouraging me to keep going when I've wanted to give up.

To the reader, thank you for picking up this book and taking a look inside. These are some of the most vulnerable, sacred thoughts & feelings that I've ever put on paper. I hope you found relatability somewhere in this creation of mine. I hope you keep supporting my journey as a writer.

Last but not least to my mother who has now passed on, thank you for telling me at 13 years old to "never stop writing", even though you never got a chance to read any of it. You saw something in me that took me years to see within myself. Your words and love are forever engraved in me.

ABOUT THE AURTHOR

Growing up in Detroit MI, Kai Alexandria always had a knack for writing from a very young age. At the age of 9, she and her family moved from Detroit to the suburbs of Romulus MI. Not too long after, at 12 she discovered her love for writing and just how much of an outlet it could be. Since then she has written countless poems and is now transitioning into professional songwriting. By publishing this collection of poetry, she hopes to inspire & encourage others to tap into their creative side and chase their dreams.

Connect with Me

https://www.facebook.com/kaialexandriapoems
https://www.facebook.com/KaiAlexandriaMusic
https://www.instagram.com/KaiAlexandria_
https://twitter.com/Kai_Alexandria

Made in the USA
Columbia, SC
30 April 2020

95114750R00065